AMERICAN ANIMALS

PAINTINGS BY
AUDUBON

EDITED BY
DORIS R. MILLER

THE GROLIER SOCIETY INC. • NEW YORK

TABLE OF CONTENTS

MOUNTAIN GOAT

THE mountain goat makes his home among the high mountain rocks. In winter, he comes down to look for grass to eat. Mountain goats often weigh up to 300 pounds.

AMERICAN BISON

THE bison is also called the buffalo. He is one of the largest animals in America. Hunters have killed so many of them that there are very few bison left in the United States today.

PRONGHORN

THE pronghorn can run very fast. He lives on the plains or in the desert. The pronghorn has very sharp eyes. He can see for many miles.

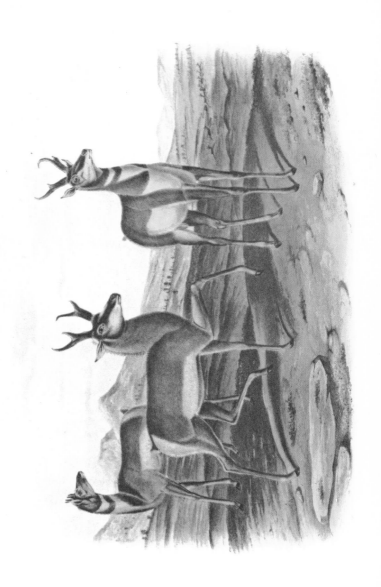

DEER

WHITE-TAILED deer live everywhere in the United States. They are protected by law. Deer feed on leaves, twigs, and fruit. They are about four feet tall and nearly seven feet long.

MOOSE

THE moose is the largest of all American deer. He can grow as large as seven feet high. He can be very dangerous. Even bears get out of his way. The moose eats lilies and other plants that grow in water.

COLLARED PECCARY

THE collared peccary is a wild pig. He eats worms, nuts, plants, and snakes. He has strong, sharp hooves, which he uses to kill rattlesnakes.

COUGAR

THE cougar is the biggest cat in the United States. He is very strong. A cougar can kill a big deer. He will hunt for many miles without any rest.

OTTER

Otters build their homes near streams and rivers. They eat fish, frogs, and turtles. They are playful and like to swim.

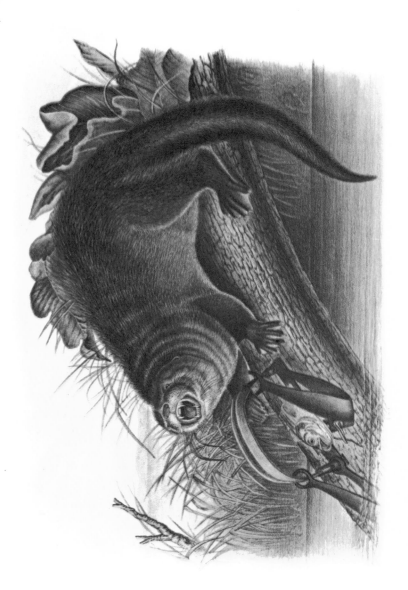

MINK

THE mink can live on land or in the water. On land he hunts rabbits to eat. When he is in the water, he eats fish and frogs. His fur is valuable for women's coats.

LONG-TAILED WEASEL

THE long-tailed weasel is brave and fierce. He likes to hunt at night. He eats mice, rats, and birds. He changes color with the seasons, becoming white in winter and brown in summer.

ESKIMO DOG

THE Eskimo dogs pull sleds over the ice and snow. They are also used for hunting polar bears. The Eskimo dog doesn't bark. He howls, just like a wolf.

BLACK BEAR

SOMETIMES the black bear can be a friend. Then he is a lot of fun. But he can also hurt people. He can climb trees and he can swim. The black bear eats fish and honey.

COYOTE

THE coyote is also called the prairie wolf. He hunts and eats rabbits and rats. In this way he helps the farmer.

RED FOX

THE red fox is full of tricks. He is hard to catch. At night he curls up on the ground to sleep.

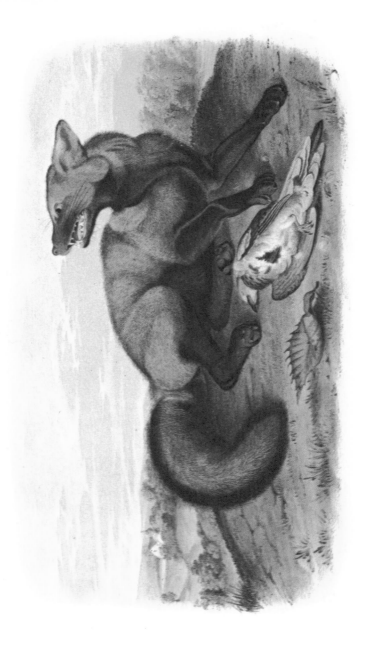

SWIFT FOX

SWIFT foxes can run very fast, but they are easy to hunt and trap. A swift fox comes out to hunt for food only at night. He eats insects, mice, and snakes.

PORCUPINE

PORCUPINES mainly live in forests. The porcupine is covered with almost 30,000 quills. Stay away from him! His quills are sharp and stick in whatever touches them.

BLACK-TAILED
PRAIRIE DOG

THE prairie dog really belongs to the squirrel family. But he barks like a dog. When danger is near, the prairie dog whistles to warn his friends.

WOODCHUCK

THE woodchuck eats and eats in the summer. Then he stays in his den all winter. He digs his den under an open field. The woodchuck is also called the groundhog.

WOOD RAT

THE wood rat likes to come out at night. He steals and hides anything he can carry. He runs along the branches of trees like a squirrel.

HUDSON'S BAY LEMMING

LEMMINGS are about 6 inches long. They look like rats. They change color from one season to another. In the winter they are white, and in the summer they are brown. Lemmings eat grass and roots.

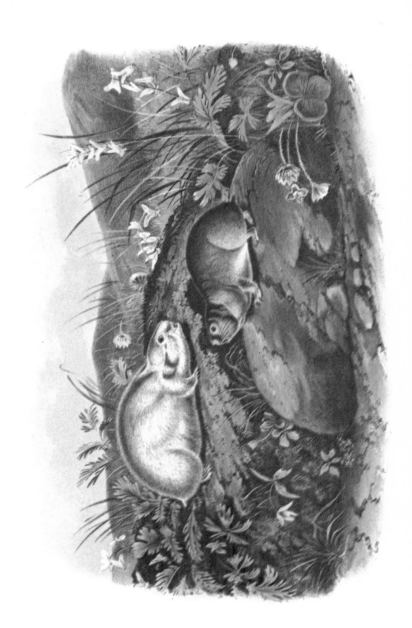

FOX SQUIRREL

THE fox squirrel does not run very fast. He lives on the edge of the forest. Here he finds his food. He likes nuts, fruit, and seeds.

FLYING SQUIRREL

FLYING squirrels do not really fly. They glide through the air from one tree limb to another. They sleep all day and hunt for food at night.

BLACK-TAILED RABBIT

THE black-tailed rabbit lives in the open country. He runs very fast and is hard to catch. Farmers don't like him because he eats the vegetables in their gardens.

SNOWSHOE RABBIT

THE snowshoe rabbit has large feet covered with long fur. They help him to travel over ice and snow. That is why he is called the snowshoe rabbit.

MOLE

A MOLE spends his life under the ground. He must dig all the time to get the food he needs. He uses his heavy claws to dig for insects, beetles, and angleworms.

OPOSSUM

WHEN an opossum is frightened, he plays "dead." He lies on the ground all curled up. He lies very, very still. When a person is very still or makes believe he is asleep, we say, "He is playing 'possum'."

SKUNK

SKUNKS help farmers everywhere. They eat harmful insects, grubs, and small animals. They give off a bad smell only when they are frightened. But you should not get too close to a skunk!

GRAY WOLF

GRAY wolves grow to be seven feet long. They usually weigh about 150 pounds. Long ago, the gray wolf lived in many parts of the country. Today, it is hard to find a gray wolf in the United States. He is found mostly in Canada.

BADGER

You can tell a badger by the white stripe that runs from his nose to the back of his head. Badgers are small animals. They have strong, long teeth and claws. They live in dens, which they dig for themselves.

JOHN JAMES AUDUBON

JOHN JAMES AUDUBON was born in Santo Domingo, in 1785. When Audubon was very young, his father took him to Paris. There he studied with the great French painter Jacques Louis David. This was the only training that Audubon ever got as an artist.

When he was seventeen, Audubon came to the United States. Audubon spent most of his life painting birds and animals. In 1838 he published his *Birds of America*. People from all over the world praised his beautiful paintings.

Audubon was finishing his book of paintings of the animals of North America when he died in 1851. His sons finished the work.

The Audubon Society is named after this great painter and naturalist.

Other Books You Will Enjoy

For information, write: Dept. PP

The Grolier Society Inc., 575 Lexington Avenue
New York, New York 10022